MW00489765

HOLD ME GORILLA MONSOON

Colette Arrand

OPO

books & objects

Opo Books & Objects
abadpennyreview.com

Hold Me Gorilla Monsoon
Copyright ©2017 by Colette Arrand
ISBN: 978-0-9973048-1-7
Library of Congress Control Number: 2017901047

Book design by Johnny Damm
Cover photograph: William M. Van Der Weyde,
Wrestling; digital positive from the original
gelatin silver negative; George Eastman Museum

For my dad, who took me to the matches,
and for my mom, who bought the tickets.

HOLD ME GORILLA MONSOON

Table of Contents

I reserve the stratosphere for me and you. And there ain't nobody else on the stratosphere. On the end of the lightning bolt that crashes through this great, vast atmosphere, Dusty Rhodes lives. I ride on the end. I've got a silver-studded saddle, and I've rode there for seven years. You've got to come up to my place.

Dusty Rhodes
"The American Dream"

I. The Use of Roland Barthes to Justify One's Love of Wrestling

The Use of Roland Barthes to Justify One's Love of Wrestling

> Leaving nothing in the shade, each action discards all
> parasitic meanings and ceremonially offers to the public a
> pure and full signification, rounded like nature.
> – Roland Barthes, "The World of Wrestling"

My mother says that she hasn't adjusted
because she has no evidence of my womanhood.
My voice is still her son's voice, my body,
however changed, is one she still pictures
as masculine. When the Freebirds blinded
Junkyard Dog with a handful of hair cream,
they prevented him from witnessing the birth
of his daughter. He required no proof;
she was born and he missed it, had to learn
the contour of his daughter's face later,
when his vision returned and he got
his revenge. I understand disbelief, the idea
that a person is so indelibly that person
that they cannot change, but as the subject
of that change I'm unable to supply proof.
Hardly wanting to seem foolish, wrestling fans
hold up the time Roland Barthes went
to the matches as proof that there's a kind

of art at work grander than the illusion
of contact. Where Barthes saw a narrative
simplification of the challenges faced
by the audience, the shook fan purchases
a kind of respect via betrayal—wrestling,
praised by a theorist, has no room
for its audience. To what standard
I'm meant to hold my entertainment
or myself to is never clear. Am I real
because I present myself as real,
or because another person recognizes
me as such? With enough study
you can learn the way a wrestler
plays to the crowd, the same way
you can learn how a woman walks
or sits or speaks. I've put these things
into practice, but I can't convince
anybody and I'm not sure I ever will.
There's a fan crying out for her favorite,
but the Junkyard Dog leaves the arena
on a stretcher. What happens next
depends on what you believe and why,
what you're given and the proof you require.

Channeling Ox Baker

You will hate me.
– T-shirt, worn by Ox Baker in the 1970s

I like to hurt people, but am no great
heart puncher. I play football and know
the way to a man's heart is to square
the shoulders and put my head
through his chest. I like to hurt people
even when I am hurt, even when
I'm barely functional with headaches,
so I study how a wrestler keeps
a sharp blade in his wrist-tape
and know every way of bleeding
so it looks like no accident.
I'm a coward and never use my skill,
choose instead a more subtle way
of destroying a body that others love.
I try to talk to my father, but we have
no way of speaking. He likes to hurt
people, too, and men who share
the language of pain are silent
with one another. In school,
I whip a classmate with my house key,

held at the end of a long chain. He begins
taking karate some afternoons. I see him
in the neighborhood wearing his gi
and understand his purpose,
but I am not afraid of him
and will beat his ass. I wish
I hadn't, that our fight had gone any way
other than its anticlimax. I wake up often
with the image of him pinning my arms back,
bearing my breast to the sky. Just once,
I'd like to sleep long enough to allow his fist
to hammer my heart, but I am the great heel
of childhood. There's never any closure
for a heel, just new territories,
new towns, the same old ways to bleed.
I do what I can to heal the scars
but they are mine. I keep them to myself.

Man of One-Thousand Holds

His tendons are taut, my objective to pull
them tighter. I am a familiar danger,
my father's capacity for violence.
When one is folded over the other,
the legs form a keyhole. From there,
the variations are infinite: threaded through,
the legs create a deathlock, the arms
a cloverleaf. The most whole
I ever felt as a man was in positions
like this, on the mat in a room learning
how to torture a man's body to a point.
You're meant to submit, ask your partner
for release. I never last as long as I'd like,
but there's a line of legs and arms to
pass through, tangling and untangling
until the mechanism is rote. I've forgotten
every hold I know, but I remember how
it felt to pass my body from one man's hands
to another, to be taken up again
and again like a cup of wine until drained.

Full Body Slam

As a child I believed my conception
was in the wake of Hulkamania,
the grapplings of my mother and father
as perfect as a skilled ring technician.
The crowd announced in Detroit is 93,173
and I believe my parents are among them
like Hulk Hogan believes his body slam
stopped Andre the Giant's heart.
But most numbers shouted into history
are falsehoods, most self-mythologizing, too.
Mom and Dad, immovable objects both,
were not stirred when Andre ripped
the crucifix from Hogan's neck, belonged
to a colony of invisible seats. I know my life
is nothing special, so I enjoy the old lies.
That Andre died instead of appearing
at five successive WrestleManias, diminished
each time. That Hulkamania lives forever.
That my father splits town and turns heel,
becomes an unstoppable force. That he
is out there still, walking from town to town
as giants walk, bringing misery and ruin.
That I am the hero of this story, that I love

the monster enough to put him down
with a slam of my own. That I put my ear
to his breast and listen for his heart
to cease its pounding. That he may rest,
his path no longer beset by those fans booing
and spitting, forever pelting him with garbage.

Executing a Pumphandle Slam

On television, it works: the wrestler
moves behind his opponent, bends him
forward, enfolds him. In the galley kitchen
of a friend's house, our first attempt
is inelegant (our arms won't thread
through his legs, our footing is nervous
around a leaping dog) and interrupted
by my partner's father. He knows
what we are doing, has seen the slam
before, but with my cock against the curve
of his son's ass, memory becomes
a foreign province. Years before *faggot*
acquires a meaning I like to self-apply,
I know that wrestling is something faggots do
with their doors closed; that some labors
are meant for private stages or no stage at all.

**In Retrospect, the Fan who Started the First "You Fucked Up!"
Chant Feels Pretty Bad About the Whole Thing**

> How ignorant thou art in your pride of wisdom!
> – Mary Shelley, *Frankenstein*

Unlike the incident in Nassau
where fans dropped a cinder block
on The Barbarian from a balcony,
his chant was innocuous,
a way of letting the wrestlers
know he was in on the joke.
The chant, drunkenly croaked
to life, outstripped its creator,
overtook a crowd all too happy
to flaunt their secret knowledge.
The chant grew, was audible
on televised events when luchadores
slipped from the top turnbuckle,
while injured men writhed
with torn ligaments. The privilege
of wrestling fandom being anonymity,
those chanting went home safely,
knowing wrestlers couldn't seek revenge.
The creator, however, went sleepless

some nights, had visions
of broken grapplers carted off
while his chant rose up
from those fans in the know.
The chant, he thought, was worse
than a wrestler's own knowledge
of failure. The chant is unaware
of the blurred line between
theatricality and crisis, cannot tell
a real paramedic from a plant
too muscular for his uniform.
It is blind to the handshake deal between
wrestler and fan: one agrees to the plausibility
of hold and counterhold, the other to pretend
the sequence mostly harmless.

For the Drunk Fan Yelling "Faggot!" at Every Heel

Roddy Piper has AIDS
– Fan sign, WWF show, 1984

I see him, burdened with the implication
of this sport, a lifetime wrapped up
in queer enterprise. Old promotions
used the same footage of a statue,
two men grappling, the action
of their muscles embellished
by the glare of studio lighting.
One man, regardless of his skill,
will be humbled by the other,
but as a straight man in an audience
of straight men, humiliation,
even by proxy, is intolerable.
The worlds we occupy ourselves with
are not real. The Russians in the ring
are not Russian; their pal, mincing
around with his silk scarves and boas,
has never taken another man's penis
into his mouth. The act is convincing
though there's nothing worth taking
shame in. We revel in the same things.

We know the secret language of flesh
and musculature. Some of us speak
it in tongues of sweat and oil.

II. Wrestling School

Illustrated by Scott Stripling

Atomic Drop

THE ATOMIC DROP IS SIMPLICITY ITSELF: A QUICK, TWO-STEP MANUEVER. LIFT AND DROP.

THE MOVE IS SO NAMED FOR THE WHITE-HOT PAIN THAT RESULTS...

...WHEN ONE MAN'S TESTICLES, IN MOTION, COLLIDE WITH THE UNMOVED KNEE OF HIS OPPONENT.

Reverse Atomic Drop

IN THE AIR, THE WRESTLER IS LIKE A COWBOY IN A FILM, RIDING HIS STEED BACKWARDS.
ONLY HERE, THE WRESTLER ISN'T SHOWING OFF. IN FACT, HE IS QUEASY.
HURF
AS HE SHOULD BE, FOR IT'S HIS DICK RIDING THAT BOMB, HIS SPIRIT THAT VAPORIZES FIRST.
HURF
POP!

Twin Magic

INITIALLY, TWIN MAGIC WAS JUST THAT: A FEAT OF MAGIC, CONJURED BY TWIN WITCHES.

THE MOVE WAS QUICKLY BANNED, HOWEVER...

WHEN IT PROVED VERY EFFECTIVE AGAINST THE PATRIARCHY.

German Suplex

INNOVATED BY PRUSSIAN SOLDIERS WHO WHERE HIGHLY SKILLED IN THE ART OF WAR...
THE SECRET OF THE GERMAN SUPLEX'S EFFECTIVENESS HAS YET TO BE DECLASSIFIED.
SAUERKRAUT
SACRÉ BLEU!
IT IS IMPOSSIBLE, HOWEVER, NOT TO ADMIRE ITS HUNDRED YEAR RECORD OF SUCCESS.
BOOMEN

Surfboard Stretch

OFF THE SHORE OF PUERTO ESCONDIDO...
A LUCHADOR WITNESSED EVENTS...
THAT HAD NADA TO DO WITH HIS INVENTION OF THE SURFBOARD.
ARRRRGH!!
HA HA HA HA HA

Irish Whip

BEFORE HE CUT THE ROPES THAT SURROUNDED THE ISLAND...
ST. PATRICK FOUND THAT ANY SNAKE HE TRIED TO THROW OUT OF IRELAND...
SIMPLY BOUNCED BACK.

Superman Punch

THE SUPERMAN PUNCH WAS SO CHRISTENED BY POPULAR KIDS...
WHO'VE CLEARLY NEVER READ ANY OF SUPERMAN'S ADVENTURES.
HMMM... WONDER IF LOIS REMEMBERED TO SET THE DVR FOR THE NEW EPISODE OF PRETTY LITTLE LIARS?
DEAR GOD!
AND TO THINK- THEY SAID THAT GEEK CULTURE WAS POPULAR!
I APPRECIATEE THE FLUIDITY OF YOUR MOVE SIR, BUT WHEN DOES SUPERMAN...
BIG DOG AIN'T GOT TIME FOR YOUR NERDBOOK!
NEXT!

The People's Elbow

WHEN LOOSED FROM ITS PAD, DWAYNE JOHNSON'S ELBOW IS QUITE CHARISMATIC.
WUT?
THE ROCK
IN HIGH SCHOOL, IT WAS VOTED "MOST LIKELY TO BE PRESIDENT OF THE UNITED STATES".
MOST LIKELY TO BE PRESIDENT
XXX
IN THAT SENSE, THE PEOPLE'S ELBOW WAS SOMETHING OF A DISAPPOINTMENT TO ITS PARENTS.
I'LL HAVE
IT DOESN'T MATTER WHAT YOU ORDER!
SIGH
ORANGE

Pop-up Powerbomb

WHILE OUT PERFORMING THE DUTIES OF A GOOD FATHER...
DAD?
KO
HUSTLE LOYALTY RESPECT
KEVIN OWENS' THOUGHTS WERE OVERTAKEN...
FRIENDS
A POP-UP ADVENTURE
POP UP!
POP UP!
MICK FOLEY
BY VISIONS OF TERRIBLE VIOLENCE!
POP!
POP!
KEVIN!

Human Torture Rack

IN A FIT OF DESPERATION...
POINK!
A MAD KING CALLED FOR THE CREATION OF THE HUMAN TORTURE RACK!
YOU CAN'T STOP NOW BROTHER!
WE'VE BEEN CALLED TO THE TORTURE!
THE RESULTING MANEUVER WAS THE BIRTH OF MODERN CHIROPRACTIC MEDICINE.
MAN, WAIT UNTIL THE EXECUTIONER GUILD HEARS OF THIS...
CRACK
YEAH! YEAH!
OH NICE

Tree of Woe

ONE NIGHT, WHILE WALKING AN UNKEMPT PATH...
A LONELY TRAVELER WAS SUBJECTED TO...
THE TREE OF WOE!
I FEEL LIKE MY FATHER NEVER LOVED ME AS A SOB SAPLING...
SIGH

Devastating Leg Drop

MOST THEORIES ABOUT MASS EXTINCTION DON'T MENTION THAT A DEVASTATING LEG DROP WIPED OUT THE DINOSAURS...
BUT IT'S NO COINCIDENCE THAT HULKAMANIA RAN A LITTLE LESS WILD...
PLEASE FORGIVE ME, BROTHERS!
HULKAMANIA
AFTER THE MESOZOIC ERA.
BA-DOOM

III. Hold Me Gorilla Monsoon

For Greg "The Hammer" Valentine and the Slow Decay of Our Bodies

The secret to the forearm is the forearm, that smashing
together of one man's flesh and another's mandible.

In a high school gymnasium, that's all you've got,
your forearm, but you're striking a much younger man

like you hate him for following in your profession,
like you hate yourself for taking up your father's.

It's hard watching you move in the ring. Your body
moves like a rock beneath a waterfall, which is to say

that your body doesn't move, but the fluid movement
of time wears down on it regardless. In your youth

you were known for your viciousness. I knew you
as The Hammer. I knew you as a man who beat

his opponents so soundly they were left partially deaf,
who broke the hero's legs and bragged about it on television.

These things live on, just barely. Sometimes a wrestler
can live so long he stops functioning as a symbol.

His forearm is just a forearm. Throw one in the ring,
break your foe's tooth. The crowd won't even know.

For Jerry "The King" Lawler, Upon Whose Behalf I Am Upset that the State of Texas Claimed the Piledriver as Its Own

The birth of *Texas*-as-adjective was an accident,
a case of machines cutting bread in slices too thick

for toasters. It no better describes the vile business
of driving a man's head into his shoulders than any other,

piledriver itself being ill-equipped. But it was you, the king
of Memphis, who perfected the maneuver, who adapted

it from phony cowboys, who utilized it as a final weapon
in defense of your city. From Hollywood, Andy Kaufman

holds a bar of soap and tells you to apply it to the skin
in circular motions. He wrestles a woman to the ground

and pounds her head against the edge of his swimming pool.
By this time it is illegal to use the piledriver in Memphis

(were they angry, as I am, about the adjective?), but the crowd
roars when you hoist Kaufman up by his waist and fall

backwards; he wins by disqualification, but how many winners
leave the arena in an ambulance? The piledriver is yours; calling it Texan

won't do. The word suggests that which is outsized and rhinestoned,
a smiling troop of Dallas Cowboys cheerleaders, not the brace

around Kaufman's neck. *Texas*: A freakshow, geeks
wearing costumes and perfuming tricks for a mark's dollar.

Sometimes a bearded lady is convincing but here her disguise
is brutal: dried glue is visible where the neck and whiskers meet.

For "Nature Boy" Ric Flair, Auctioning Off His NWA World Heavyweight Championship

I remember your brag that a good pair of alligator shoes
cost more than a house. What do those shoes now satisfy?

Can the soul be minted tender? Can blood? These are what you have
to offer now. Both things are spoiled, but they're yours to give.

At bars, you are paid to drink. At baseball games, the same.
You tell stories about drinking with old friends. Are they not here?

A Rolex watch, a private jet, one night with a perfect woman:
All things you say I cannot have. But I have had you, and still can.

Walk the aisle for me Nature Boy, until you're no longer able.
I will let you rest. I will swaddle you in a sequined robe.

For Jake "The Snake" Roberts, on the Occasion of Making an Unlikely Out in Centerfield During a Charity Softball Game

Like every catch before or since, yours is a matter of geometry
and probability. To say this is to admit that I believe in miracles.

Professional wrestling is the work of death and resurrection. I watch
to see your throat cut. To see you rise, nearly ruined. Over and over.

In your documentary's climax, you are smoking crack in the bathroom.
You show me this to articulate that some men prefer ruin.

Again the gambler crows that he has twenty-two. The game
is blackjack. Few are born to cast lots, but who does this stop?

For the Ultimate Warrior, Screaming Nonsense Into the Void

> Queering doesn't make the world work.
> – Warrior, to a heckler at his speech to the College Republicans of
> the University of Connecticut, April 5, 2005. This statement cleared
> up his remark that "queers [weren't] as legitimate as
> heterosexuals."

You spoke to me, tasseled Achilles, through the pop
and distortion of video cassette. First exposure to language.

When we speak of homosexuality now, we do so softly.
Not you. Tolerance! As if life were tolerable. As if difference.

For you we imbibe a synthetic nostalgia,
a tonic to forget your old betrayals.

You were unchanged in a changing world, but why?
If queering won't make this world work, what will?

I would like to be your censor, Warrior. The only one.
When I speak your name into empty spaces, you fill them.

For Dwayne "The Rock" Johnson, Positioned Just So Across From Vin Diesel

In this film I can queer you
without much imagination.

You are uncoupled, surrounded
by men, each an expert with a pistol

grip, tense and longing
to be unburdened. There's Vin,

squinting at the beef on his grill.
The Victorians had chairs that sat

two lovers the way you are now blocked.
I saw one of these in a museum

and asked why two people in love
would sit like that. We live

in an uncertain space where sex
between men is public and nervous.

One man fucks another with his eyes first,
then agrees to fuck either there

or in private. We're told it's different now,
but you two won't leave the barbecue.

You're just excited to be seen with a man—
you hardly need to touch in the dark.

For Hulk Hogan, Who, By His Own Reasonable Estimate, Has the Largest Arms In the World

In a bookstore, I saw Atlas figured on the covers of innumerable
paperbacks and thought of you. Brother, the burden those arms

must carry. The work of lifting giants, quelling earthquakes,
and cupping the noise of the mob to an ear is yours;

you asked for it then and you ask for it now. Your arms I imagined
variously: the jack pressing a car over my father's body, the cranes

in my mother's factory, twin pythons that could devour my problems
were I able to scream your name loud enough. I screamed,

but I won't see you in the flesh until that flesh, no longer taut,
is incapable of its former glories. Until then, I invent my own encounters

and spin those. Here is one: once, I claimed to have met you
at a Big Boy restaurant, pouring syrup on a stack of pancakes.

When you took my hand in yours, it disappeared. Then you did.
I need you to cup your ear, Hulk. Tonight, when I call out, come.

For Brutus "The Barber" Beefcake, Unable to Cut Hair

It should have been obvious: hedge shears cannot navigate
the part in a man's hair with any accuracy, are useless

in matters relating to the crew cut, the mop top, or the short
regular. It was the bowtie, maybe, or the tassels on his biceps

alternating red and white like a barber pole, his zeal
for the mullets of other men. My barbers never smelled

of baby oil, never used anything larger than a pair of scissors.
Their shops were open, buildings tangible and lived in.

Brother Bruti's was a prop, a sugarpane window disgruntled wrestlers
hurled their enemies through. He often stood back from fistfights,

hiding among his empty anticeptic jars, ducking behind
his flophouse barber chair. His eyes were those of an empty man,

eyes I recognized as my own. Desperately, we clung
to our fictions, even when nobody was there to pay attention.

In old pictures I am bald, my hair shaved down to the scalp.
I used to pay for rough treatment, a razor scraped

down the nape of my neck. Brutus said he loved his blades
and needed to use them. A man in a national guard armory

allows himself to be put to sleep, his hair trimmed, scattered
on the mat. I did this too, to feel another man's caress.

For The Great Muta, Who, By Massaging an Extra Gland in the Back of His Throat, Is Able to Spray a Fine Poison Mist

In middle school, I listened to Madonna sing about the hardships
of being a woman and wept because I couldn't know them.

I try telling my mother how I feel, that I hate my cock and would lose it
so my desires could have an acceptable outlet. Where I got this idea

I don't know—Divine, maybe, speaking candidly about her happiness
not requiring a sex change. The world I'm detailing is beyond my mother

and she evaluates me the way a movie scientist evaluates a monster
of her own making: mystified. We put this behind us, but I eventually

unmask before either of us are ready. How else can I explain?
If only my difference were as obvious as The Great Muta's, a clutched

throat, a blinding green mist. I've often wished for an extra organ, something
tactile and sensuous. A piece of myself I could hide if it meant living pleasurably.

For CM Punk, Finished With Professional Wrestling

I have always been suspicious of strangers, but you
are known to me. I can outline your every bruise.

I am naïve, prone to falling for simple tricks
or passing kindness. A hand here. A word.

You aren't saying anything and I need to be fine
with silence. You paid for this ride; you don't need to speak.

You leave like an unfulfilled lover, the subject
of a failed aubade. It is winter. The bed is cold.

Men are a fact of my life until they aren't.
You are strange to me now. Of you, I know nothing.

For "Adorable" Adrian Adonis, Unable to Wash the Pink From His Hands

> Hey A.D., which way is the wind blowing today, brother?
> Have you taken a walk on the wild side in awhile?
> – Hulk Hogan, 1986

In the midst of an epidemic you emerge
from your closet, trade in your leathers

for silk scarves as if one could make you
more or less of a queen. When you die,

it is not because of your blood; you go
in a car wreck, bereaved by your wife

and remembered by a journalist
as a brawler on the verge of rehabilitation,

a wrestler ruined by his culture's need
for someone to play the fag. Adrian,

for a week I felt called out by a series
of photographs of gay men and the clothing

they wear: denim jacket, denim jeans, flannel
button-up, and a pair of Converse: Basic Gay.

Thumb dug into a beltloop and back against
the wall, I guess he's what you'd call

vanilla, but that's how a gimmick functions
in the real world, like a secret language

nobody teaches but all the right people know.
When you speak, I hear a man pretending

to know desire. You kiss a man and he faints,
but you're only trying to win a match.

In the locker room your makeup runs
in the shower like blood from a wound,

but not everything that you scrub will come
clean. I can read the marks you bear, speak

the shame you know but can't articulate.
Like you, I approach men looking to be made

whole in their embrace. I can read these marks
to you as well. In fact, we share them.

Acknowledgements

My thanks to the following journals, in which variations of these poems first appeared:

491 Magazine, Hobart, KNOCKOUT, BOAAT, Whiskey Island, Moonsick Magazine, Big Lucks, and *Vanilla Sex Magazine.*

My thanks to Karen Craigo, Nathan Riggs, and A.A. Balaskovits, who saw the potential in what I was doing before I did, and to Raquel Salas-Rivera, Ginger Ko, and Moss Angel Witchmonstr, all of whom make me incredibly grateful to be a poet.

My thanks to Scott Stripling, without whom *Wrestling School* would have been impossible. His keen eye and animated pencils brought the most out of my scripts.

My thanks to Johnny Damm for designing and publishing this collection.

My thanks to James Adomian, from whose album *Low Hangin' Fruit* I took the title of this collection.

My thanks to Ed Blair, Robert Newsome, and Caroline Schmitt, who put up with my wild theories and ridiculous claims, and too many people in the community of wrestling fans to list.

Finally, my thanks to Chris, John, Aaron, Rickey Shane Page, Veda Scott, Grado, and the rest of the Clevo wrestling crew, who gave me a home in the sport I love and let me know I still had one when I needed it.

About the Author

Colette Arrand is a transsexual from Dearborn, Michigan. Her work has appeared in *The Offing, The Toast, The Atlas Review*, and elsewhere. Her first chapbook was *To Denounce the Evils of Truth*. She is the founding editor of *The Wanderer*.

About the Artist (*Wrestling School*)

Scott Stripling is an artist and illustrator living in Athens, Georgia. He publishes comics and zines under the Shoot the Moon Comics label. His work has appeared in *Gigantic Sequins, Hobart, The Atomic Elbow*, and elsewhere. His website is scottstriplingart.com.

CPSIA information can be obtained
at www.ICGtesting.com
Printed in the USA
LVHW101541130819
627499LV00009B/314/P